Disneyland®

THE FIRST QUARTER CENTURY

"To all who come to this happy place: welcome. Disneyland is your land. Here age relives fond memories of the past... and here youth may savor the challenge and promise of the future.

"Disneyland is dedicated to the ideals, the dreams and the hard facts which have created America... with the hope that it will be a source of joy and inspiration to all the world".

WALT DISNEY

Inscription on plaque dedicated July 17, 1955
Town Square, Main Street, U.S.A.

WHAT is Disneyland? For more than a quarter of a century, more than 200 million guests from nearly every nation have visited Walt Disney's Magic Kingdom to find out for themselves. But Disneyland offers no definitive answer, because no two people leave the Magic Kingdom with exactly the same memories, experiences or impressions.

Disneyland is a kaleidoscope of unique entertainment forms. It represents the intangibles of the mind, yet exhibits a logical, physical world. Within its thematic realms are medieval castles and rocket ships, horse-drawn streetcars and streamlined monorail trains, jungle elephants and elephants that fly, a snow-capped mountain and a "space" mountain.

Disneyland's Main Street, U.S.A. brings to life the spirit of America at the turn of the 20th Century, while Tomorrowland looks ahead to the turn of the 21st. America's heritage is found in rugged Frontierland and Bear Country, and in the grace and charm of New Orleans Square. The sleeping dreams of childhood are awakened within the courtyard of Fantasyland's fairytale castle. Within the dense tropical jungles of Adventureland, dreams of far-off, exotic places come to life.

Disneyland is the innocence of youth and the wisdom of age. A child examines the hitching posts that line an 1890 street and asks, "Mommy, what kind of parking meters are these?" An elderly gentleman on the same street smiles happily and tells a bystander what he likes best about Disneyland—"I can jaywalk here!" A young man aboard a "Mississippi" stern-wheeler on a moonlit night seeks an introduction to a girl by asking, "Is this your first trip abroad?"

"I don't want the public to see the world they live in while they're in Disneyland. I want them to feel they're in another world."

Disneyland is a place where people forget their everyday cares and immerse themselves in lands of fantasy and adventure, yesterday and tomorrow. You find the magic of Disneyland in the soft pastel lighting on "Sleeping Beauty Castle" as evening approaches, in the dancing eyes of a grandfather wearing an orange-billed Donald Duck hat, and in a child kissing Mickey Mouse while Dad fumbles with his camera.

Disneyland is the emotion that wells up within you when the "Mark Twain" stern-wheeler churns 'round the bend, twinkling with pin lights from stem to stern, while nearby a Dixieland band blasts out "When the Saints Go Marching In." It is the pride you feel when the band renders the "Star Spangled Banner" at the Main Street Retreat Ceremony each evening, as a flock of white doves encircles Town Square.

But to describe the real meaning of Disneyland is to unfold its story from the very beginning—from the time when it was merely a twinkle in the eye of its creator. It is to Walt Disney, "Showman of the World,"* that we dedicate this tribute to his Magic Kingdom.

*Walt Disney was named "Showman of the World" by the National Association of Theater Owners in 1966. He is the only person to have been so honored.

From
Dream
to Reality

THE TWENTY-YEAR DREAM

In the *Minneapolis Tribune* shortly after Disneyland opened, Will Jones wrote: "If it's an amusement park, it's the gosh-darndest, most happily-inspired, most carefully-planned, most adventure-filled park ever conceived. No ride or concession in it is like anything in any other amusement park anywhere."

Disneyland was obviously never meant to be a traditional "amusement park." Dedicated on July 17, 1955, the new concept in entertainment was much more—a fabulous playground, something of a fair, a fairytale kingdom, a metropolis of the future. Above all, it was a place for people to find happiness and knowledge.

When Disneyland opened in Anaheim (27 miles southeast of downtown Los Angeles), it was a 20-year dream come true for Walt Disney, its creator, chief architect and head "Imagineer." Early "descriptions" of Disneyland are on file at the Walt Disney Archives dating back to the 1940s.

"Disneyland really began," Walt said, "when my two daughters were very young. Saturday was always 'Daddy's Day' and I would take them to the merry-go-round and sit on a bench eating peanuts while they rode. And sitting there, alone, I felt that there should be something built, some kind of a family park where parents and children could have fun together."

So, in his "spare time" between films and other projects, Walt Disney began to dream and plan a new kind of family entertainment center.

Members of his staff recall Walt talking about building a "magical little park" adjacent to his Burbank movie studio. It was to be about eight acres in size, with pony rides, "singing" waterfalls, a train and statues of Mickey Mouse, Donald Duck, Pluto, Goofy and other famous Disney characters alongside which visitors could pose for pictures. It would be a place to be enjoyed by studio tours, and where Disney employees might spend relaxing weekends picnicking with their families.

Walt Disney with daughters, Diane and Sharon.

Walt Disney Studios in Burbank, California, and an artist's rendering of the "magical little park" that Walt originally envisioned to be built nearby.

But this was just a beginning idea and it would have to wait—there was too much work to be done elsewhere. World War II intervened and the Disney animated characters "enlisted" to star in a variety of training and morale films to be viewed by millions of American and Allied servicemen.

The "magical little park" idea was far from forgotten. In fact, in the ensuing years the concept was becoming more "magical" and less "little." Soon designs for themed architecture were being worked into the plan to give it more flavor. And it was becoming clear that eight acres, although fine for a few pony rides, would be too small a space to hold Walt Disney's dream.

By the early 1950s, concepts for the project had outgrown any available land space near the Disney Studio. By now, the project was evolving into something that would require a major amount of capital, and few people other than Walt and his brother Roy had faith that this bold new idea would ever break even—let alone make a return on the investment.

"I could never convince the financiers that Disneyland was feasible," Walt recalled, "because dreams offer too little collateral." *Newsweek* magazine reported that "to build Disneyland, Walt and his brother Roy Disney borrowed to the corporate hilt, and then Walt sold his vacation home and borrowed against his personal life insurance policies."

In early 1954, 180 acres of Anaheim orange groves waited to be transformed into a "Magic Kingdom."

Collectively, some of the people who were most indifferent and reserved toward the Disneyland concept were the nation's amusement-park owners and operators. Early in 1954, key Disney staff members assigned to Disneyland development toured major amusement parks across America, learning far more about what *not* to do than what to do. Recalls one: "We could have paid for the entire trip with a few dollars from each person who told us, 'If you don't put in a roller-coaster or a Ferris wheel, you'll go broke!'"

A family park? A park without "whips" and "shoot-the-chutes"? A park *sans* barkers, baseball-throws and a tunnel of love? Top amusement-park owners couldn't believe it. "All of that money just for theming and landscaping? Walt's got to be kidding. It'll never go!"

But Walt Disney wasn't discouraged by the negative comments. "It was as though Walt had a crystal ball," said a Disney executive. "If the bankers or other people in show business didn't know what he was driving at, Walt just figured they didn't understand—and went right ahead with his newest idea because he personally believed in it. He was never off on 'Cloud Nine,' yet he never did something merely because he

thought it would be a commercial success. Every project had to be one that Walt himself felt would be fun to create."

In the final analysis — beyond the usual Disney perseverance and stubborn belief in a good idea—the financial catalyst in bringing Disneyland to reality was television. Just when all remaining doors appeared to be closed, Walt Disney Productions and the American Broadcasting Company signed a seven-year contract that called for Walt to produce a weekly, one-hour television show.

Unlike the many motion-picture producers who viewed television as a threat to their entertainment organizations, Walt Disney saw the new medium as an ally. It would be a natural way to bring the story of the Magic Kingdom into the homes of millions of American families. The name for this new show would, of course, be "Disneyland."

The television show made its debut in fall 1954, and the magic of Disney entertainment immediately became a household event across the nation. More importantly, there was finally enough money to make Disneyland, the themed "entertainment world," a reality.

"IMAGINEERING" THE DREAM

The land, as Walt Disney remembered, was all flat — no rivers, mountains, castles, or rocket ships — just 180 acres of orange groves and a few acres of walnut trees in Anaheim, California.

Because it had no precedent, there would be no simple solutions in Disneyland's design and construction. Everything would be one-of-a-kind. And yet, the uniqueness of Walt Disney's concept was nearly equaled by the uniqueness of the "imagineering" team he formed to help make his dream a reality.

How to make believable wild animals, recreate a Mississippi paddle-wheeler, build a turn-of-the-century "hometown," design a Bavarian castle and send a

rocket to the moon, were questions never before encountered by an entertainment staff.

The creative demands that would be placed on WED Enterprises (an acronym for Walter Elias Disney) would call for a harmonic blend of talents unequaled in the annals of the entertainment industry. There would be artists, sculptors, designers, architects, engineers, story tellers, special-effects experts and many others.

In order to find most of these talents, Walt turned to the field he knew best — motion pictures. And in many cases, he selected the people he knew best, those already skilled in the Disney approach to family

Detailed scale models were a key part in the "Imagineering" of Disneyland.

WED artists' early renderings of two "themed" areas in Disneyland—
Adventureland and Main Street's Town Square.

entertainment. Key members of his own studio staff had open eyes and open minds for new ideas.

One Disney designer recalled, "When we began designing Disneyland, we looked at it just as we do a motion picture. We had to tell a story, or in this case a series of stories. In filmmaking, we develop a logical flow of events or scenes that will take our audience from point to point through a story.

"If we were to 'leapfrog' from Scene One to Scene Three, leaving out Scene Two, it would be like sending the entire audience out to the lobby for popcorn in the middle of the film. When they came back, how could we expect them to understand what was happening?

"There was another thing we had to keep in mind in developing our Disneyland 'story.' In filmmaking, although we can control the sequence of events, the viewer might walk in late and, through no fault of our own, miss Scene One and never catch up to the story.

But in Disneyland, we had more control. We designed the entire Park so that a guest couldn't miss Scene One or Two. From the moment he entered our 'theatre,' that is, our front gate, Scene One would begin for him."

Thus, in Disneyland's design, everything would be a form of storytelling. The Disneyland audience would not simply sit before a motion-picture screen. They would physically experience an adventure, seldom as spectators, but almost always as "participants" in the drama.

As Disneyland's design evolved, two important considerations were always kept in mind — maintaining the theming of each area and ensuring easy access.

For decades, world's fairs and amusement parks had been confusing "nightmares" of environmental design. Each show or pavilion competed for the visitor's attention like billboards along a highway. There

First rendering of Disneyland sketched in 1953.

were "Wild West" shows next to circus acts next to international exhibits — a potpourri of visual contradictions entangled in a maze of criss-crossing streets and sidewalks. The result ultimately left visitors disoriented, sometimes lost, exhausted and often unreceptive to the ideas presented, or to the idea of ever coming back.

Disneyland's design was unprecedented. Rather than competing, five distinctly different themed areas would complement each other to contribute to the total guest experience. "Scene One" was **Main Street, U.S.A.,** where turn-of-the-century America would be relived. Walt Disney wrote, "Many of us fondly remember our small hometown and its friendly way of life at the turn of the century. To me, this era represents an important part of our nation's heritage. On Main Street we have endeavored to recapture those by-gone days."

Here is America from 1890 to 1910, at the crossroads of an era. Here the gas lamp is giving way to the electric lamp, and a newcomer, the sputtering "horseless carriage," has challenged Old Dobbin for the streetcar right-of-way. America was in transition; the discoveries of the late 19th Century were changing our way of life.

"For those of us who remember the carefree times it recreates, Main Street will bring back happy memories. For younger visitors, it is an adventure in turning back the calendar to the days of grandfather's youth."

At the end of Main Street, fanning out from a central hub like spokes in a wheel, were the other "lands" — easy to find, easy to enter, each a complete thematic experience bringing to life many of Walt Disney's greatest filmmaking endeavors.

Adventureland: (Based on the popular Disney True-Life Adventure films.) "The spirit of adventure is often linked with exotic tropical places. Many of us dream of traveling to these mysterious, far-off regions of the world.

"To create a land that would make this dream reality, we pictured ourselves far from civilization, in the remote jungles of Asia and Africa. The result is Adventureland, 'the wonderland of nature's own design.'"

Frontierland: (Recreating the pioneer days of Davy Crockett and frontier America.) "All of us have cause to be proud of our country's history, shaped by the pioneering spirit of our forefathers. It is to those hardy pioneers, men of vision, faith and courage, that we

16

have dedicated Frontierland. Here you can return to frontier America, from the Revolutionary War era to the final taming of the great Southwest. Our adventures are designed to give you the feeling of having lived, even for a short while, during our country's pioneer days."

Fantasyland: (Bringing Walt Disney's famed cartoon characters to life in storybook attractions.) "When we were planning Fantasyland, we recalled the lyrics of the song, 'When You Wish Upon a Star.' The words of the melody, from our picture 'Pinocchio', inspired us to create a land where 'dreams come true'.

"What youngster, listening to parents or grandparents read aloud, has not dreamed of flying with Peter Pan over moonlit London, or tumbling into Alice's nonsensical Wonderland? In Fantasyland, these classic stories of everyone's youth have become realities for youngsters—of all ages—to participate in."

Tomorrowland: (An entertaining look at the marvels of the future.) "Tomorrow can be a wonderful age. Our scientists today are opening the doors of the Space Age to achievements that will benefit our children and generations to come.

"In Tomorrowland, we've arranged a preview of the wonderful developments the future holds in store. You will actually experience what many of America's foremost men of science and industry predict for the world of tomorrow.

"The Tomorrowland attractions have been designed to give you an opportunity to participate in adventures that are a living blueprint of our future."

On July 21, 1954, ground was broken for the Magic Kingdom and a one-year race against time began. There were times when the stumbling blocks inherent to the project appeared insurmountable. One man remembers tagging the orange trees to be saved with

Clearing the land at the Anaheim site (looking north), the triangular perimeter of Disneyland begins to take shape.

Nearing Opening Day, the "Rivers of America" begin to "flow" through a fledgling wilderness.

strips of red paper, and those to be removed with green paper. As fate would have it, the bulldozer operator was color-blind.

A construction supervisor recalls his glow of pride as water flowed into the Rivers of America in Frontierland for the first time, and his feeling of desperation as it promptly disappeared into the sandy soil of the former orange grove. After experimenting with plastic and other substances, clay soil was finally trucked in to "waterproof" the leaking riverbed.

But the dream was indeed slowly becoming reality. Disney landscape architects replaced orange trees with tropical jungles and pine forests. There were also the formal floral gardens of Gay '90s America and whimsical miniature versions of medieval European countrysides, including a giant "patchwork quilt"

Though not quite ready for the waters of the Jungle Cruise, twin hippos seem to be sharing Walt's smiling demeanor.

Above, back-to-back buildings from two different "lands"—Main Street and Adventureland—share one roof designed to reflect the two unique themes.

of flowers and shrubs. "Walt Disney depleted our nurseries from Santa Barbara to San Diego," wrote Hedda Hopper, the prominent Hollywood columnist.

Once the plants were in place, Disney landscape architects strove to make them look like they had always been there. They were protected with massive doses of "TLC"—tender loving care—as cement, cobblestones, logs, bricks, steel and nearly every other building material known sprang up around them in thousands of shapes and sizes. There were castles and cottages, a fort and cabins, rocket ships and miniature freeways, streetcars and horseless carriages.

But not all the action was confined to the building site. For the design and development of Main Street, U.S.A. alone, hundreds upon hundreds of books, pictures, historical magazines and other items were studied to get a strong feeling for the atmosphere of a typical small town at the turn of the century.

A treasure hunt extended across the country into antique stores, private homes and out-of-the-way junk shops in small towns. Scouts tracked down relics of the past ranging from old lighting fixtures to well-worn hitching posts. There were small park benches from San Francisco and grillwork and railing from old plantations in Nashville and Memphis. When important equipment could not be found in good working order, such as horseless carriages and stern-wheelers, they were handmade from the ground up by Disney craftsmen at the Studio.

Through painstaking attention to detail, the Disneyland decor began to blossom. Walt Disney had become totally absorbed in his project, and when not at the Studio supervising the attractions' development, he was walking "the site" (as it came to be called), making suggestions and spreading enthusiasm.

The architectural style of Sleeping Beauty Castle is a composite of French and Bavarian castles from the Middle Ages. The 75-foot tall spires appear to be even higher through the visual technique of forced perspective, with larger stones placed at the castle's base, and progressively smaller ones toward the top.

Castles, jungles, and rivers begin to replace orange trees and sand flats in early 1955.

A 19th Century Main Street is born again, with the ground floor buildings designed on a 9/10 scale, and the second and third stories progressively smaller... again, forced perspective at work.

Ruth Shellhorn, a consulting landscape architect for Disneyland, reflected on Walt's continual "changes of heart," in an article for *Landscape Architecture:* "I doubt if this procedure could have been followed successfully on any other project on earth. But this was Disneyland, a sort of fairyland. And Walt's belief that the impossible was a simple order of the day so instilled this spirit in everyone that they never stopped to think that it couldn't be done—they just did it, with amazing speed."

Walt Disney would occasionally be dissatisifed with his staff's designs and would take over an attraction's planning himself. In the concept for Tom Sawyer Island, Walt felt that the artists had misunderstood the idea, and so one evening he took home the plans.

By the next morning, he had designed the whole shoreline basically as it exists today.

Along Main Street, U.S.A., there would be a not-so-subtle difference between the buildings and a movie set. The latter is to be seen but not touched or entered by the audience — its structure being a mere facade behind which little or nothing exists. In contrast, Main Street and the other four lands would be worlds to be entered, of sights and sounds, touch and smell — of three-dimensional realities. In truth, this Main Street

The 76-foot high "Rocket to the Moon" is hoisted onto its launching pad.

would also be quite unlike the real Main Streets of yesteryear. Everything would always remain fresh and new. The rows of old-time ships, vehicles, and all the other elements would function together in harmony unlike anything grandfather had ever experienced. As one Disney Imagineer put it, "This is what the real Main Street *should* have been like."

These architectural and aesthetic aspects of Disneyland were not its only significant innovations. An unprecedented training and development program was initiated with the opening of the "University of Disneyland" at the Anaheim site. A hand-picked staff of future "Disneylanders" majored in the fine art of "creating happiness," and received a special curriculum in human relations and Disney philosophy.

Disneyland was sealed from the "outside world" for good when a 20-foot earthen berm rose up around the Magic Kingdom. Tracks were laid on the berm to carry 1890-style passenger trains on a grand-circle tour of the property. This was the one and only holdover idea from the original "magical little park" concept of two decades before—a train ride.

The Lilly Belle Grows Up

The Lilly Belle, a model train that once huffed and puffed around the backyard of Walt Disney's Holmby Hills home, was the prototype for the most letter-perfect re-creation of an 1890 railroad train that ever whistled into a Main Street station.

Walt's little locomotive, ⅛ full-scale, was first "blown up" in drawings, then made into a plywood mock-up large enough for a man to walk through. When it was determined that a six-foot door was adequate for a human passenger, the rest of the design followed in proportion. The size of the door dictated the size of the

roof, the sides, and finally the wheels — 36 inches apart on the tracks, or almost exactly the same width as the narrow gauge railroads of old.

The Disneyland Railroad cars followed, proportionately speaking, the Lilly Belle's example. Two trains, an 1890 passenger and a western freight train, were constructed in the machine shop at the Disney Studio. Each train was painstakingly designed and assembled piece by piece. Finely detailed wood, metal and iron-work and most parts were individually crafted in the Disney machine shop. The two trains, named C. K.

Walt's life-long love of trains initially resulted in a scale model that wound through the backyard of his home in Holmby Hills.

Walt delighted in showing his "Carolwood-Pacific Railroad," as it was called, to friends and relatives alike. A curious young nephew examines the "Lilly Belle," the train's engine.

GROWN UP...Walt's "Lilly Belle" model served as the prototype for the most letter-perfect re-creation of an 1890 locomotive that ever whistled into a Main Street station...the "E. P. Ripley."

Holliday and E. P. Ripley, were built specifically for Disneyland in 1954-55 and both have 4-4-0 engines. (They have four wheels in front, four drive wheels, and no trailing truck or tender.) Two rebuilt engines were later added to the Disneyland Railroad, an 1891 model from Louisiana and a 1925 version from New England.

Walt Disney's lifelong love of trains was expressed in the Disneyland Railroad. His backyard toy had "grown up," and now he could share with the world another of his childhood fantasies. His interest dated back to his teenage years when he "rode the rails" selling candy and newspapers on trains rolling between Kansas City and Chicago.

PIECE BY PIECE...the 105-foot long, 150-ton
Mark Twain stern-wheeler was transported to
Disneyland and assembled at its own dry dock on
the Rivers of America. The ship's hull was constructed at a Long Beach shipyard, while the body
was built at the Disney Studio.

Opening Day Draws Near

As Opening Day drew near, the Disney staff worked around the clock to ready this new "show" for its world premiere. Even the horses were rehearsing. For four hours each day, they pranced around a ring, while music, tooting automobile horns and laughter and shouts of crowds blared at them from loudspeakers. Amongst the Opening Day guests, the horses would feel right at home.

At the Studio, Imagineers were building many of the show elements that were to be transported to Disneyland piece by piece. One of the finest examples was the Mark Twain, a 105-foot long, 150-ton stern-wheeler. The ship's hull was constructed at a Long Beach shipyard, while the body was built on the Studio lot. One deck at a time, the structure was trucked down the Santa Ana Freeway and assembled at its own dry-dock on the Rivers of America.

One by one, the other "scenes" of the Disneyland show were completed, and finally Walt Disney's persistent idea — his "new concept in family entertainment" — was ready for its world debut. The "magical little park" had become a $17,000,000 "Magic Kingdom." And the dream had at last come true.

During its first summer season alone, Disneyland welcomed more than half a million guests.

With a trumpeter's fanfare, excited children follow Disney characters across the drawbridge of Sleeping Beauty Castle, the gateway to Fantasyland.

A World Premiere

"I think that everyone here will one day be as proud to have been at *this* opening as the people who were there at the dedication of the Eiffel Tower." An excited Bob Cummings was talking to a television camera. The actor was one of the many video "stars" of the day who were gathered for the 90-minute grand dedication. It was July 17, 1955, and it was live coast-to-coast network television. The applause was real. There were no canned laughs, no studio magic tricks, and no editing miracles at hand to save any miscues.

Art Linkletter, the prominent radio and television personality, walked through the first castle to be constructed this side of the 17th Century and temporarily lost his microphone. Trying to regain his composure, he nervously introduced Captain Hook and his crew of pirates as "Captain Crew."

Comedian Alan Young spun madly about in a giant-sized teacup, while Jerry Colonna, another comic, clung to the controls of a "runaway" Casey Jr. Circus train. Danny Thomas rode a horseless carriage right back through time to the turn of the century, and Frank Sinatra and Sammy Davis Jr. drove along a miniature version of "tomorrow's freeway."

AND THE BAND PLAYED ON...
On Opening Day, Bandmaster Vesey Walker posed with the original 16-piece Disneyland Band. Their tremendous popularity extended a "temporary" two-week engagement...to over 25 years! Although the musicians have changed, the Disneyland Band continues to be one of the Park's favorite "attractions."

As Walt dedicates Fantasyland, the drawbridge of Sleeping Beauty Castle is lowered.

Below, Jerry Lewis is the "kid" on Mr. Toad's Wild Ride, and Irene Dunne yells "We're listing…!" as she christens the Mark Twain.

Entertainer Sammy Davis Jr.

Original Mouseketeers (Annette, Cubby and Karen in foreground) join the jamboree.

Ronald Reagan, Bob Cummings and Art Linkletter discuss TV show details prior to their live coast-to-coast broadcast.

Roy Rogers, Dale Evans and family watch the Main Street Parade.

Buddy Ebsen, Fess Parker and Art Linkletter introduce a "new frontier" to a national TV audience.

Nearby, Fess Parker as Davy Crockett — already a national hero on Walt Disney's year-old television show — was riding through newly planted pine forests in premature answer to a gunshot that was misfired on camera. Actress Irene Dunne christened the beautifully constructed Mark Twain riverboat with a bottle of water from American rivers, then immediately declared "We're listing!," as an overflow crowd poured on board. And at one point, Walt Disney himself accidentally appeared on camera ahead of schedule, talking to one of the TV crews manning 22 cameras and straining to capture the excitement of it all.

Prominent roles were also played in the festivities by then California Governor Goodwin Knight and future President Ronald Reagan. But Walt Disney, future "Showman of the World," played the greatest role. This was his finest moment — a triumph for a man who had dared to dream and boldly reach out beyond his contemporaries. It was also a moment of truth for his critics, who had predicted that his unique idea would be a "Hollywood Spectacular — a spectacular failure." Other pundits had christened it "Disney's Folly."

The telecast was delightfully spontaneous, exhibiting the freshness and honesty of live video coverage in its early days. Although the humorous miscues were held to a minimum, the number of stars, celebrities and public figures on hand seemed almost endless. It was a grand premiere unlike anything Hollywood had ever seen.

Walt Disney, California Governor Goodwin Knight and President of the Santa Fe Railroad, Fred Gurley.

"I don't want the public to see the world they live in while they're in the Park," Walt Disney said. "I want them to feel they are in another world." And with that he dedicated Disneyland:

"To all who come to this happy place: welcome. Disneyland is your land. Here age relives fond memories of the past and here youth may savor the challenge and promise of the future.
"Disneyland is dedicated to the ideals, the dreams and the hard facts which have created America…with the hope that it will be a source of joy and inspiration to all the world."

The First Quarter Century

*D*ISNEYLAND has become an international symbol of happiness and inspiration…a living showplace of beauty and magic filled with the accomplishments, joys and hopes of the world. More than 200 million "children of all ages" have enjoyed Walt Disney's Magic Kingdom, including kings, queens, prime ministers and presidents. Through the years, Disney "Imagineers" have added new shows, attractions and themed "lands," while improving original ones. As Walt promised, "Disneyland will never be completed as long as there is imagination left in the world." Although the future holds the promise of even more dreams come true, the first 25 years at Disneyland marked an unforgettable era. From the first young children to enter "Sleeping Beauty Castle," to the dedication of the newest adventure— "Big Thunder Mountain Railroad" —the following pages represent a "family album" recapturing special moments that helped to make Disneyland "The Happiest Place On Earth."

Dorothy Lamour, "on the road to Disneyland."

The Main Street "White Wing," Trinidad, was one of the most photographed "characters" in Disneyland.

UNDER THE BIG TOP…The Mickey Mouse Club Circus "came to town" on Thanksgiving Day, 1955. Although it included the first live appearance by television's Mouseketeers, the overall Circus did not have the uniqueness of the other Disneyland shows, and was discontinued in early 1956.

A REAL RECORD BREAKER…
Disneyland's longest-running show, the "Golden Horseshoe Revue," has been a popular "hitching post" for audiences since Disneyland's Opening Day. With five shows daily, it's little wonder that the Revue is listed in the *Guinness Book of World Records* as the longest-running show in history—with more than 43,000 performances.

CAPTAIN NEMO'S NAUTILUS...The actual submarine set from the popular Disney movie, "20,000 Leagues Under the Sea," was exhibited in Tomorrowland, complete with the Giant Squid.

The Mouseketeers' biggest, most lovable member, Roy Williams, was often found sketching in Tomorrowland.

"THE CHRISTMAS BOWL" captured the spirit of the Yuletide season with music. One of the earliest holiday presentations at Disneyland, the "Christmas Bowl" featured scores of local youth bands, choral groups and orchestras as well as Disneyland's own Charles Dickens Carolers.

PHANTOM BOATS, AUTOPIA FREEWAY, ROCKET TO THE MOON and a "spaceman" exemplified the "world to come" in Disneyland's Tomorrowland '55.

ADVENTURELAND, I PRESUME? Although hardly recognizable by today's standards (no Enchanted Tiki Room, no Tahitian Terrace), the intrigue of far-off islands and tropical jungles attracted Disneyland's first visitors by the thousands.

Two native Californians exchanged greetings over the Disneyland Stagecoach Line (then Vice President Nixon was a frequent visitor to Disneyland), while Conestoga wagons, pack mules and stagecoaches gave a continual demonstration of frontier "rapid transit."

AND THE STARS CAME OUT…
Dinah Shore and husband George Montgomery join Walt Disney at the wheel of the Mark Twain; Jimmy Stewart takes "one last look at civilization" before departing on the Jungle Cruise; Alan Ladd and family arrive in Frontierland aboard the Disneyland Railroad; and two "sad sacks"—Milton Berle and Jerry Lewis—wait patiently for some grownup to claim them.

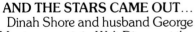

A LABOR OF LOVE…One of the most delicate, picturesque realms in Disneyland—Storybook Land—was introduced in Fantasyland during the first years of the Magic Kingdom. In fact, this tiny childhood world was one of Walt's personal favorites.

Model makers at the Disney Studio labored six months turning artists' visualizations of Pinocchio's Village, the straw-stick-brick homes of the Three Little Pigs, and other fabled favorites into detailed buildings. On a scale of one inch to a foot, they fashioned lead hinges so six-inch doors would actually open for electricians to change light bulbs. Tiny toys were carved for the window of Geppetto's shop, and "stained glass" and leaded windows were handcrafted and installed.

When the miniature dwellings were complete, landscapers brought the village to life by the ingenious use of plants and flowers. After selecting plants whose leaf size was but little more than a quarter inch, they further restricted growth by planting them in containers. A three-foot tall Japanese Boxwood, with gnarled trunk, was shaped and pruned to represent the oak tree where Alice entered the Rabbit Hole. A 100-year-old grapevine was uprooted and turned upside down to appear like the "terribly tortured old snag" in front of Ratty's home from "Wind in the Willows." Finally, a "magical" growth retardant was added to all the trees and shrubs to further restrict growth to no more than one inch per year.

In 1956, the **RAINBOW CAVERNS MINE TRAIN** wound its way through rocky, desert landscapes filled with cacti and precariously balanced boulders. The climax of the adventure was the multi-hued waterfalls cascading through the Rainbow Caverns.

The same year, the **SKYWAY** became the first aerial tramway of its kind in the United States, and was opened by Walt Disney and Swiss Counsel General of Los Angeles, Dr. Walter Schmid.

Special guests of 1956 included Charles Laughton and his wife, Elsa Lanchester; Joe E. Brown; and Chief Justice Earl Warren and family.

"FANTASY IN THE SKY"...1956 marked the beginning of Disneyland's traditional summer nightly pyrotechnics display. Today, the Magic Kingdom has become one of the largest users of fireworks in the world.

EXPANDING THE FRONTIERS...
Tom Sawyer Island opened to the public in June of 1956, and was dedicated by Walt and two youngsters from Hannibal, Mo., representing (who else?) Becky Thatcher and Tom Sawyer.

FORT WILDERNESS, like Frontierland's entrance stockade, was constructed from logs hewed by hand and trucked in from nearby mountains. The timber was floated across the "Rivers of America" and hoisted up to dry land, where it was assembled to create the realistic 19th century army fort.

The **INDIAN VILLAGE** in Frontierland displayed ancient Indian customs and crafts, while entertaining guests with authentic dances from such tribes as the Apache, Navajo, Commanche and Pawnee. All dances were performed with the permission of the respective tribal councils and the U.S. Bureau of Indian Affairs.

Some 7,500 celebrants welcomed in 1958 as part of Disneyland's first annual **NEW YEAR'S EVE PARTY.** Today's New Year's Eve parties attract over 25,000 guests each year.

A MINIATURE VERSION OF TOMORROW'S HIGHWAY...the Autopia Freeway opened in Tomorrowland. "Kids" big and small raced over bridges and under tunnels at a "top speed" of 11 m.p.h.

V.I.P.'s AT HOME AND ABROAD...

King Mohammed V of Morocco was welcomed
to Disneyland personally by Walt Disney in 1957.
After the King and his entourage arrived back at
his hotel, his Highness slipped past his body-
guards and returned to the Magic Kingdom
incognito, wishing to see it again through the
eyes of the average tourist.

Former President Harry
Truman, finding it hard *not* to
be recognized, also enjoyed a
visit to Disneyland.

In mid-1957, Monsanto's **HOUSE OF THE FUTURE** opened to show Tomorrowland visitors how the innovative use of plastics could shape our homes of tomorrow. The result of three years of planning and design, the cantilevered plastic shell enclosed a five-room living environment complete with furniture—and almost everything made out of plastic materials.

The **VIEWLINER,** Tomorrowland's predecessor to the Monorail, often found itself alongside a living reminder of its "coal-burning" past.

SLEEPING BEAUTY AWAKENS…What more appropriate personality for the opening of a fairy-tale castle than the little princess herself, Shirley Temple (Black)! In 1957, the famous Disneyland landmark opened up its interior passages to reveal a delightful three-dimensional portrayal of the story of Sleeping Beauty.

COLUMBIA, "GEM OF THE KINGDOM"

A full-scale replica of the first ship to carry the American flag around the world, Disneyland's Columbia was christened June 14, 1958.
The ten-gun, three-masted ship was designed from plans and photographs supplied by historical and governmental groups. With the exception of its hull (which was trucked in from a Long Beach shipyard), the proud windjammer was constructed entirely at Disneyland.

Her creation was the result of a conversation between Walt and the manager of Frontierland, as they were casually observing the water traffic on the "Rivers of America"—the Mark Twain, two Mike Fink Keel Boats, two Tom Sawyer Island Rafts and three Indian War Canoes. "Look at that," Walt remarked to his companion. "Now there's a busy river." The other man expected him to complain about the congestion. Instead, Walt continued, "What we need is another BIG boat!" And thus was born the Columbia.

GUY WILLIAMS, known to millions as the masked champion Zorro, entertained Disneyland guests with swashbuckling duels and perilous swordfights.

Comedian **DANNY KAYE** showed he had complete faith in his "chauffeur" as he abandoned the wheel of his Autopia car.

Disneyland's "Old Fashioned Automobile Parade" made its debut on Main Street, U.S.A., enhancing the nostalgia of a bygone era.

THE MAGIC OF CHRISTMAS FILLS THE MAGIC KINGDOM

Since the first "Christmas Bowl" in 1956, the Yuletide season has always been a major Disneyland celebration. But the most dramatic of all the Christmas festivities is, perhaps, the inspiring "Candlelight Procession." Premiering in 1958, this parade of carolers illuminates the Magic Kingdom with the glow of a thousand candles and the music of a thousand voices. Over the years, some of Hollywood's most respected performers have participated in the finale of the "Candlelight Procession"—the reading of the Christmas Story. These celebrities have included John Wayne, Henry Fonda, Cary Grant, Charlton Heston and Gregory Peck.

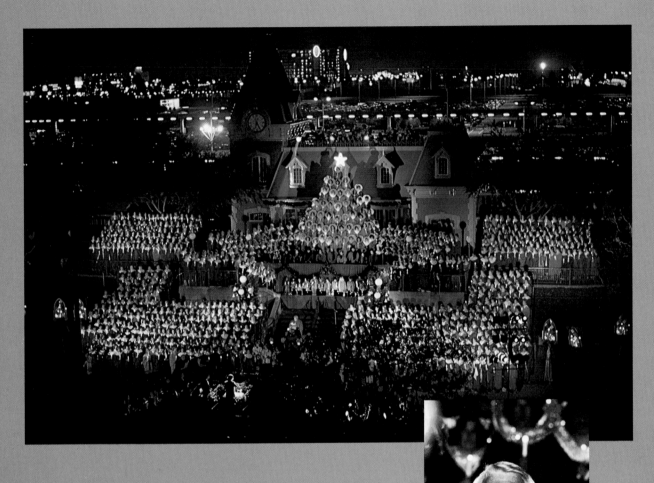

CHRISTMAS DREAMS COME TRUE

Christmas time at Disneyland has traditionally been highlighted by special holiday parades. Each year a magical procession of Christmas dreams "comes to life" with the help of dozens of artists and technicians and more than 200 performers.

The Park's Yuletide flavor is enhanced with bountiful holiday dressings, including a garland-draped Main Street and a 60-foot Christmas tree adorned with over 3,000 lights and ornaments.

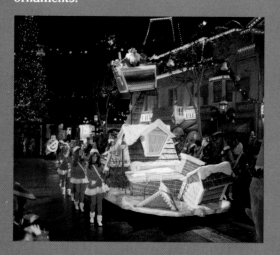

Disneyland WELCOMES 1966 GRADUATES

GRADUATES CELEBRATE AT THE MAGIC KINGDOM…A unique concept in graduation commemorations, the popular "Grad Night" parties were introduced by Walt Disney in 1961 when he invited 8,000 students from 28 Los Angeles area high schools to celebrate their commencement at Disneyland.

Since then, "Grad Night" parties have become a tradition, featuring top-name entertainment. Nearly two million high-school seniors from all over the United States have culminated their high-school careers with the all-night graduation celebration at Disneyland.

A GRAND OPENING FOR A GRAND CANYON...1958 welcomed the world's longest diorama, Disneyland's re-creation of the flora and fauna of Arizona's great abyss. At the dedication ceremony, 96-year-old Hopi Indian Chief Nevangnewa blessed the trains that would carry visitors past the dramatic diorama.

ALICE IN...FANTASYLAND
That mischievous white rabbit who led Alice astray made amends by presenting the fairy-tale blonde with the key to Fantasyland's newest adventure, Alice in Wonderland. When not at Disneyland portraying Lewis Carroll's famous character, this "Alice" was Mouseketeer Karen Pendleton.

A MOUNTAIN COMES TO ANAHEIM...

In the early months of 1959, a new form slowly emerged on the Orange County horizon. Residents could hardly believe that a mountain was actually "growing"...but there it was... in full view of the busy Santa Ana Freeway: Disneyland's own Matterhorn.

As was the case with many Disneyland attractions, the Matterhorn was born from the script of a Disney motion picture. In this case, the impetus was supplied by the film, "Third Man on the Mountain," which was inspired by Walt's love of Switzerland and his fascination with the legendary mountain.

Soon, Walt was making plans for a speeding bobsled adventure that picked up where the movie left off, a chance for the audience to experience firsthand the icy slopes of a Disneyland Matterhorn.

Numerous photographs of the Swiss peak were carefully studied to create the most accurate replica possible. Scale models led to blueprints, which eventually unfolded into lath, plaster, rebar and cement. The final result is a perfect 1/100th scale re-creation of the famous Swiss peak.

**TOMORROWLAND'S
TRANSPORTATION GOES ABOVE
AND BELOW**…As the snowy
peaks of the Matterhorn neared
completion in 1959, Tomorrowland
saw the addition of several major
attractions and adventures, including
the Monorail and the Submarine
Voyage.

Since the early days of Disneyland,
Walt had wanted to include a "train
of the future." After much research
and study, Disney engineers returned
from Cologne, Germany, where they
had been impressed by an experi-
mental monorail developed by the
Alweg Company.

After recommending the system
to Walt, Disney designers joined with
the Alweg staff in 1958 to develop a
basic plan that would lead to a
working prototype. From there, the
trains were designed and built at the
Disney Studios in Burbank, and the
Disneyland Monorail became the first
passenger-carrying system of its kind
in the Western Hemisphere.

Inspired by the 1954 Disney classic,
"20,000 Leagues Under the Sea,"
a fleet of eight realistic submarines
also found a home in Tomorrowland.
Although his designers had originally
suggested a glass-bottom boat ride,
Walt wasn't satisfied. "No," he said,
"let's give them a real submarine ride.
We'll take them down in the water
and let them look out of portholes…
giv'em a real show!" With that,
$2,500,000 was "submerged" to
create the fascinating world of liquid
space.

Becoming one of the world's largest peacetime fleets of submarines, the hulls for the eight subs were built by the Todd Shipyards of San Pedro, and then completed at the Disneyland Naval Yard. Technical data and advice were supplied by the General Dynamics Corporation, a firm closely associated with America's operating nuclear submarines.

THE "HIGHWAY IN THE SKY" IS OPENED…In June of 1959, Vice President Richard M. Nixon and family helped Walt Disney introduce his new Monorail system to a world audience. The .8 mile-long beamway would later be lengthened to 2 1/2 miles to reach to the Disneyland Hotel and back.

The Monorail, Submarine Voyage and the Matterhorn, along with the expansion of several other existing attractions, represented an investment of $6 million.

V.I.P.'s…NATIONAL AND INTERNATIONAL

By the end of the decade, Disneyland had gained such national attention that the *Christian Science Monitor* suggested that it was "almost an instrumentality of American foreign policy." To this, Walt Disney replied, "We love to entertain kings and queens, but at Disneyland, everyone is a V.I.P."

At Disneyland in the 1960's, distinguished guests included: Senator John F. Kennedy with Guinea's President Sekou Toure, King Bhumibol of Thailand, California's Governor Edmund "Pat" Brown, Edward Kennedy and King Hussein of Jordan.

ONE V.I.P. WHO "ALMOST" MADE IT TO DISNEYLAND…

When Nikita Khrushchev, the Premier of Russia, visited the United States in 1959, he expressed his desire to see Disneyland. At a film industry luncheon attended by scores of movie stars, he was advised that too many security precautions were necessary before he could visit the Magic Kingdom, and that he would not be able to go. Like a child who had been denied a toy, the Soviet leader ranted, "Just now I was told that I could not go to Disneyland. I asked, 'Why not? What is it? Do you have rocket launching pads there? I do not know.' And just listen, just listen to what I was told, to what reason I was told. 'We,' which means the American authorities, 'cannot guarantee your security if you go there'."

His voice began to shake and his face turned darker. "That is the situation I am in—your guest. For me, the situation is inconceivable; I cannot find the words to explain this to my people!"

This "international incident" set off immediate responses from around the world: Author Herman Wouk wrote, "I don't blame Khrushchev for jumping up and down in a rage over missing Disneyland; there are few things more worth seeing in the United States, or indeed anywhere in the world."

Bob Hope quipped, "Here we are in Alaska, our 50th state. Alaska—that's halfway between Khrushchev and Disneyland!"

And in New York City the day following the incident, an officer of a large brokerage firm telephoned a Disney executive to say, "Maybe you don't remember me; I'm the one who said we don't finance 'kiddylands' when you were looking for money to build Disneyland. Now I want to visit your place; if Khrushchev can get so mad over *not* seeing it, Disneyland can't be much of a kiddyland!"

GETTING BACK TO NATURE
Walt and his not-so-sure-
of-herself granddaughter,
Tammy, began the inaugural
Pack Mule Ride through
Nature's Wonderland.

Passengers on the Mine Train
found the thundering waterfalls
of Cascade Peak to be a "wet
and welcome" beginning during
hot summer days.

Based on Walt Disney's True-Life
Adventure films, the Mine Train
Through Nature's Wonderland
featured a "cast" of more than
200 animated birds, reptiles and
animals in their natural habitat.
After more than a year and a
half in development, the popular
adventure opened in 1960. It
included the spouting "Old
Unfaithful" geyser and the spectacular, phosphorescent waterfalls of Rainbow Caverns.

MAKING WISHES COME TRUE…Children representing countries from all around the world helped Walt dedicate the Snow White Wishing Well and nearby Grotto at the side of Sleeping Beauty Castle. Coins dropped by "well-wishing" guests have benefited international children's charities for years. The figures in the background of Snow White and the Seven Dwarfs were sculpted in fine Italian marble by European craftsmen.

IDENTIFIED FLYING OBJECTS…flying saucers *did* land…in Tomorrowland, 1961. These unique, air-cushioned vehicles attracted "astronauts" of all ages as they hovered over the space station platform, sometimes "intercepting" one another.

BABES IN DISNEYLAND…During the 1961 Christmas season, the Babes in Toyland Village made its debut on Disneyland's Main Street. Named after the newly released film, the actual giant-sized studio sets were used to create a fairy-tale setting.

JUST WHISTLIN' DIXIE…1961 celebrated the
second anniversary of "Dixieland at Disneyland," a
musical spectacular upon the waters of the "Rivers of
America." To introduce the talents of over 50 jazz musicians, "Satchmo" Louis Armstrong led the production
from a raft especially constructed for the occasion.

Disneyland featured its own "house" Dixieland bands at the river show, which included the Firehouse Five Plus Two, the Disneyland Strawhatters and the Young Men from New Orleans. The "Young Men" featured vocalist Monette Moore and a quintet of veteran jazz players; Joe Darensbourg, clarinet—Johnny St. Cyr, banjo—piano man Harvey Brooks—drummer Alton Redd and trumpeter Mike Delay.

By contrast to the experienced musicians playing at the park in 1961, a new group of "unknowns" made their professional debut at Carnation Gardens...the Osmonds.

FAMILIAR FACES BEGIN THE '60's…"At the wheel" of several popular attractions…former President Dwight D. Eisenhower and his wife, Mamie, became "honorary members" of Disneyland's Fire Department. Entertainer Johnny Cash piloted the Mark Twain, while India's Prime Minister Nehru "safely returned to civilization" on the Jungle Cruise.

DISNEYLAND'S "FLYING HOSTESS"...For Disneyland guests, the highlight of any summer evening was Tinker Bell's flight from Sleeping Beauty Castle, and the dazzling "Fantasy In The Sky" fireworks spectacular.

Actually, Tinker Bell made her Disney debut in the 1953 animated version of Sir J. M. Barrie's classic, "Peter Pan." A year later, she became the charming hostess of the Disney TV series, and in 1961, the famous pixie was introduced at Disneyland in the person of 71-year-old Tiny Kline, a former Ringling Bros. aerialist.

Several years later, Tiny handed her wand and wings to 19-year-old Mimi Zerbini, a French circus acrobat, who herself was succeeded by Judy Kaye. Tinker Bell "flew" from 1961 through 1977.

ADVENTURELAND'S "FAMILY HIGH RISE"

From the pages of Johann Wyss's novel, "Swiss Family Robinson," came the 1961 Disney film of the same name. One year later, the Swiss Family Treehouse literally "grew" to life size in Adventureland.

The tree used six tons of reinforced steel and 110 cubic yards of concrete in construction. With over 300,000 handmade vinyl leaves and blossoms, the 80-foot high wonder weighed almost 150 tons when it opened to Disneyland visitors.

MORE ADVENTURE IN ADVENTURELAND...

In 1962, an entire pool of frolicking Indian elephants brought the new Disney process of "Audio-Animatronics" to the Jungle Cruise. Complementing this addition was the opening of the tropically themed Tahitian Terrace Restaurant, where the "Royal Tahitians" performed beneath the spreading limbs of a huge "Disneydendron."

While inspecting this mammoth tree of cement limbs and artificial leaves, Walt gazed from the rear terrace of the restaurant and commented, "You can't see the show from here...the foliage is in the way. Let's do something about it." When his engineers confessed that it would be virtually impossible to raise the creation without great expense, Walt suggested that they simply add six feet to the trunk. The trunk was cut near the base, six extra feet of reinforced steel and cement were added—and the problem was solved!

A STAR IS BORN…A strangely familiar man in red and white was seen directing the installation of the 24-foot Christmas star in 1961. The sparkling decoration shone from atop the Matterhorn for many years before being retired as part of Disneyland's energy conservation efforts.

AN UPLIFTING EASTER…"Rising to the occasion" on Easter Sunday, 1962, the colorful balloon from the motion picture "Around The World In 80 Days" left Disneyland's Plaza following a traditional old-fashioned Easter parade down Main Street.

**1963 PERSONALITIES PLAY
AT THE MAGIC KINGDOM**
Clockwise: Sophia Loren,
Jack Benny, Martha Raye.

GETTING INTO "THE SWING"...Ever since Benny Goodman first performed at Disneyland in 1961, the Magic Kingdom has played host to a variety of Big Bands. In 1963, Walt Disney personally presented some of these Big Band leaders with miniature piano-radios, honoring their talents and marking Disneyland's first "Cavalcade of Big Bands." From left: the Elliot Brothers (Bill and Lloyd), Lionel Hampton, Charlie Barnet, Gene Krupa and Les Brown.

Other "greats" of the Swing Era that performed at Disneyland included Harry James, Count Basie, and Duke Ellington.

SPACE-AGE ENTERTAINMENT COMES TO THE MAGIC KINGDOM...

In the early '60's the word "Audio-Animatronics" was born from a somewhat old Disney idea. Through the years, Walt had intermittently toyed with the thought of using animated, three-dimensional characters at Disneyland. At one time, in fact, he hoped to include a Chinese restaurant featuring a Confucius-style mechanical man who would spout Oriental words of wisdom. His very early forms of "Audio-Animatronics" made their appearance in the Jungle Cruise and Nature's Wonderland. The Enchanted Tiki Room, however, represented a whole new era of this sophisticated form of entertainment.

In essence, the process of "Audio-Animatronics" electronically synchronizes and combines voices, music and sound effects with the movement of animated figures. By 1963, this computerized system had exploded into a magnificent obsession, and plans for an Enchanted Tiki Room—overflowing with the color and spirit of the islands—were quickly put into motion.

In its original concept, the Enchanted Tiki Room was envisioned as a restaurant, with an after-dinner performance by a group of beautiful birds. But it was decided that this "dinner and show" combination would not be practical for Disneyland, and so the restaurant idea was dropped and the feathered entertainers were expanded to create an entire show.

THE COLUMBIA "OPENS UP" A NEW SHOW...In 1964, Frontierland's three-masted windjammer offered guests a closer look at her past when the below-decks quarters were opened. Walt and Admiral A. C. Richmond inspect the cook's section, filled with antiques and replicas of equipment from the 18th century.

...AND THE JUNGLE CRUISE BECOMES MORE "PERILOUS"...Never content with the status quo, in 1964, Walt and his "Imagineers" again surveyed the regions of "darkest Africa" just two years after the addition of the Elephant Bathing Pool. This time, an African Veldt was added and filled with a variety of "wildlife," big and small.

"I just want to leave you with this thought…that it's been sort of a dress rehearsal and we're just getting started. So if any of you start resting on your laurels, I mean just forget it, because…we're just getting started."

WALT DISNEY
1965 Tencennial Celebration

Disneyland's ten-year anniversary was celebrated with the dedication of one of the Park's most momentous and dramatic accomplishments…Great Moments with Mr. Lincoln. Previewed at the 1964-65 New York World's Fair, the amazing production was brought to Disneyland where it has fascinated audiences ever since.

For the first time, Disney technicians were called upon to create a "human" performer …an "Audio-Animatronics" figure which would simulate human movements realistically, and which would preserve the delicate dignity of a "Presidential" presentation.

At right, Walt Disney and a WED designer discuss the finishing touches on a scale model of the show.

A BIT OF THE BAYOU COMES TO DISNEYLAND

In July of 1966, New Orleans Mayor, Victor Schiro, joined Walt Disney for the opening of New Orleans Square. The three-acre, $18 million expansion authentically captured the winding streets, iron-laced balconies and the intimate shops and courtyards of the famous Louisiana city a century ago. A New Orleans reporter covering the story quipped, "It's the next best thing to being there…"

…AND *IT'S A SMALL WORLD* OPENS TO THE WHOLE WORLD

One of Disneyland's most renowned and best-loved attractions, *It's A Small World,* really has proved to be "the happiest cruise that ever sailed." One of the four Disney-designed shows at the New York World's Fair, the attraction features more than 500 "singing and dancing" dolls representing children the world over.

Walt advises Bank of America Board Chairman, Louis Lundborg (Bank of America presents *It's A Small World* at Disneyland) on the construction progress. At the dedication ceremonies, Walt was surrounded by appropriately dressed children from around the world.

ON THE ROAD AGAIN…While enroute to join Disneyland's 50th adventure, Primeval World, this Tyrannosaurus Rex startled more than one freeway motorist. But despite all the horn honking and heckling from passers-by, the 22-foot "Audio-Animatronics" monster completed the trip unscathed to become a part of this dramatic adventure.

Walter Elias Disney passed away on December 15, 1966. Here he pauses for a picture with his lifelong friend...the last photograph of Walt and Mickey together.

It would take more time than anybody has around the daily news shops to think of the right thing to say about Walt Disney.

He was an original; not just an American original, but an original, period. He was a happy accident; one of the happiest this century has experienced; and judging by the way it's been behaving in spite of all Disney tried to tell it about laughter, love, children, puppies and sunrises, the century hardly deserved him.

He probably did more to heal or at least to soothe troubled human spirits than all the psychiatrists in the world. There can't be many adults in the allegedly civilized parts of the globe who did not inhabit Disney's mind and imagination at least for a few hours and feel better for the visitation.

It may be true, as somebody said, that while there is no highbrow in a lowbrow, there is some lowbrow in every highbrow.

But what Walt Disney seemed to know was that while there is very little grown-up in a child, there is a lot of child in every grown-up. To a child this weary world is brand new, gift wrapped; Disney tried to keep it that way for adults…

By the conventional wisdom, mighty mice, flying elephants, Snow White and Happy, Grumpy, Sneezy and Dopey— all these were fantasy, escapism from reality. It's a question of whether they are any less real, any more fantastic than intercontinental missiles, poisoned air, defoliated forests, and scraps from the moon. This is the age of fantasy, however you look at it, but Disney's fantasy wasn't lethal. People are saying we'll never see his like again.

Eric Sevareid
CBS Evening News
December, 1966

A GREAT, BIG BEAUTIFUL TOMORROW

"Now, when we opened Disneyland, outer space was Buck Rogers. I did put in a trip to the moon. And I got Wernher von Braun to help me plan the thing. And, of course, we were going up to the moon long before Sputnik. And since then has come Sputnik and then has come our great program in outer space. So I had to tear down my Tomorrowland that I built 11 years ago and rebuild it to keep pace."

WALT DISNEY, 1966

Walt Disney often commented that the one aspect he appreciated most about Disneyland was that it was something he could "keep building, keep plussing and adding to." No better example of that revamping and reshaping can be found than in the $23,000,000 rebirth of Tomorrowland in 1967.

By the mid-1960's, the astronauts and the advances of science and industry had caused Walt's original Tomorrowland to become "todayland." The time for change had come.

The true impetus for Tomorrowland's face-lift came as a result of the 1964 New York World's Fair, in which "Audio-Animatronics" had come into its "technological own," and where Disney had established a unique relationship with American industry. Walt's idea from the beginning was to move it all (all the Disney shows) to Disneyland. And, the place to start was with General Electric's Carousel of Progress.

The four-act, six-theatre revolving building was a great success at the Fair, but there was just no room for it at Disneyland. Here was the final catalyst from which was born the plans for a new Tomorrowland... a home for the Carousel of Progress.

With Mickey Mouse—space helmet and all—more than 1,500 celebrities and invited guests attended the dedication of the new Tomorrowland in 1967.

Two innovative vehicles were introduced to Tomorrowland in 1967 in the form of the "Atomobile," transporting guests through the new Adventure Thru Inner Space, and the PeopleMover transportation system which illustrated a possibility for rapid transit of the future.

The Flight to the Moon adventure lost a rocket but gained a Mission Control Center as part of its new 1967 look. Here, the "Audio-Animatronics" Operations Director, "Mr. Morrow," gives Disneyland guests a preview of what to expect in their lunar voyage.

Another returning feature of Tomorrowland was the America the Beautiful Circle-Vision Theatre. This attraction began its Disneyland career in 1955 as "Circarama, U.S.A." but obtained the "America the Beautiful" title when it went on the road to the Brussels Fair in 1958. (One version traveled a total of nine years under the auspices of the U.S. Information Agency.) Other versions of Circle-Vision were produced by the Disney studio for "Italia '61" Exposition *(Circling Italy with Circarama)* and an exposition at Lucerne, Switzerland *(Magic of the Rails)*. "America the Beautiful" was reshot for the opening of the new Tomorrowland (and has since been updated again).

YO HO...YO HO...In the late 1950's, Walt Disney introduced the concept of a pirate adventure to his staff at WED. Like so many other Disneyland dreams that eventually became reality, the idea for a pirate show was far ahead of the technology required to achieve the desired effects. It was not until the middle 1960's that the Pirates of the Caribbean show could move forward toward actual realization. The research, story development and actual construction of the pirate adventure in New Orleans Square required several years and the expenditure of millions of dollars.

A Disney artist sketches one of the many scenes of the Pirates of the Caribbean. Drawings such as this eventually evolved into a unified tale in pictures called a "storyboard."

From the renderings, intricate scale models were built. Complete with miniature props and costumed pirate figures, the models were finely detailed... from facial expressions to hinges on the treasure chests! These scale models enabled Disney "Imagineers" to view the adventure as guests would later see it.

A PIRATE'S LIFE FOR ME…In the Spring of 1967, the rowdiest crew of black-hearted swashbucklers who ever plundered the Spanish Main "came to life" in the thrilling "Audio-Animatronics" adventure. Today, the Pirates of the Caribbean stands as one of the finest examples of the art of "Imagineering"—the blending of creative imagination with technical know-how.

ON THE CAMPAIGN TRAIL...The 1968 Presidential campaign brought a host of candidates to Disneyland in the summer months: Alabama Governor George Wallace, Senator Robert Kennedy from New York who was accompanied by former astronaut John Glenn, and former Vice President Richard Nixon.

★ ★

Ethiopian Emperor Haile Selassie gets the "royal treatment" on his tour of Disneyland.

WHEN HINGES CREAK IN DOORLESS CHAMBERS…For six years, the distant, ominous Haunted Mansion stood unoccupied upon the New Orleans shores of the Rivers of America. A sign posted in front offered passers-by a once-in-a-lifetime invitation…

> "Notice! All ghosts and Restless Spirits…post lifetime leases are now available in the Haunted Mansion! Don't be left out in the sunshine. Enjoy active retirement in this country club atmosphere—the fashionable address for famous ghosts, ghosts trying to make a name for themselves…and ghosts afraid to live by themselves! Leases include licenses to scare the daylights out of guests visiting these happy haunting grounds. For reservations, send resume of past experience to: Ghost Relations Dept., Disneyland.
>
> "Please! Do not apply in person!"

And soon the letters came, from many parts of the world. There was the nine-year-old who wrote, "On Halloween, I help in a spook house at our school," and the 12-year-old who claimed to have "scared my mom clear out of her wits." And the frustrated New England spinster, chagrined because "not one of my neighbors believes in witches…ANYMORE." Walt Disney once remarked, "We'll keep up the grounds and things outside, and the ghosts can take care of the inside."

ONE SMALL STEP…The arrival of Apollo 11 on the surface of the moon was an historic milestone for Disneyland as well as the world. This was the Park's first REAL moon landing, televised on the Tomorrowland stage to a throng of fascinated Disneyland guests.

…AND ONE GIANT PRODUCTION
The following year, the Tomorrowland Stage hosted the fast-paced musical comedy, "Show Me America." More than 120 sparkling costumes were made for the production, which featured favorite American melodies sprinkled with a touch of old-fashioned humor. From its premiere performance, when 60 members of the press led a standing ovation, through its summer-end closing 124 performances later, the show was acclaimed by audiences and critics alike.

A HUNDRED-MILLION SMILES
Miss Valerie Suldo, a 22-year-old
New Brunswick, New Jersey
payroll clerk, became Guest Number
100 million at 11:13 a.m. Thursday,
June 17, 1971, launching a
summer-long celebration.

...BUT THE LOSS OF A BROTHER

*"My job all along was to help Walt to do the things he wanted
to do. He did the dreaming; I did the building."*

Roy O. Disney

Three months after he dedicated Walt Disney World to his late
brother, Roy Disney passed away on December 20, 1971.

Co-founder of Walt Disney Productions, Roy added the
essential complement to Walt's creative genius. He provided
the financial wizardry which made it possible for dreams like
Disneyland to become a reality...to survive and grow. Roy's
business acumen not only carried out the dreams of his brother,
but put the entire Disney organization on sound financial ground

In 1966, Roy Disney inherited the worldwide Disney company through the untimely death of his brother, Walt. Throughout the busy years that followed, he was completely dedicated
to building Walt's dream. Roy was the keeper of the flame...
the curator of the spirit that Walt Disney created.

ELECTRIFYING ENTERTAINMENT…

One of the most beautiful and unusual pageants to glitter its way down Main Street premiered in 1972 as one of the highlights of Disneyland's summer nighttime entertainment. Winding its way through the Park, the "Main Street Electrical Parade" dazzles guests with a half-a-million tiny, twinkling lights depicting fanciful scenes from Walt Disney film classics.

It required nearly a hundred artists and craftsmen to create the sparkling, battery-powered parade floats, some measuring up to 14 feet high and 75 feet long. The unusual music, electronically produced, is transmitted to each float's amplifier/receiver, which broadcasts the melodies in a unique and unprecedented sound system. The "Main Street Electrical Parade" would, by popular demand, become bigger and brighter for many years to come.

ALL-AMERICAN DISNEY BAND...In the summer of 1972, the strains of a vibrant, rhythmic musical aggregation could be heard permeating the air of the Magic Kingdom. This vivacious group, the "All-American College Band," was a new addition to the Park's summertime entertainment program, and has been greatly enjoyed by the Disneyland audience ever since. As part of the "Disney Entertainment Work Experience Program," these college musicians are given the opportunity to perform before millions of people, while at the same time completing their educations. When not entertaining Disneyland visitors, the band (and a newer group, "The All-American College Singers") can be found in the classroom learning the tools of the trade taught by renowned artists in the entertainment industry.

Senator Hubert Humphrey celebrated his 61st birthday at Disneyland.

POOH IN '72...After hosting presidential candidates for years, Disneyland sponsored its own hopeful campaigner in the form of lovable Winnie the Pooh. Unfortunately, Winnie didn't make it to the White House, but in his concession speech he paraphrased Walt Disney, "Who wants to be president when you can be king of Disneyland?"

JAMBOREE…COUNTRY BEAR STYLE…It was a spring day in 1966. With several new projects on the drawing boards, including the enormous Walt Disney World in Florida, Walt Disney had begun a typical process—tossing out ideas to see what would "grow."

"Why don't we try something with bears?" Walt suggested to several designers and story men. "Yeah, a bear band, you know, to play music and things…" Almost six years later, in 1972, Country Bear Jamboree opened an extended run in Disneyland. It was the hit show of Disneyland's seventh land, the wilderness land of Bear Country.

HENRY LEARNS HIS LINES…Teaching a bear to do tricks is one thing, but rehearsing the furry animal through musical medleys and humorous one-liners can be an almost un-bear-able experience.

THE WALT DISNEY STORY opened at Disneyland in 1973, and represents the Magic Kingdom's special salute to its creator.

THE LIFE...AND LEGEND OF WALT DISNEY

The creator of Mickey Mouse and founder of Disneyland, Walt Disney possessed one of the most prolific imaginations the world has known. He won more than 950 honors and citations from nearly every nation, including 32 Academy Awards and five "Emmys." His personal awards include honorary degrees from Harvard, Yale, the University of Southern California and UCLA; the Presidential Medal of Freedom; France's Legion of Honor and *Officer d'Academie* decorations; Thailand's Order of the Crown; Brazil's Order of the Southern Cross; Mexico's Order of the Aztec Eagle; and the "Showman of the World" award from the National Association of Theater Owners.

Walt's career began in the early 1920s, when he left Kansas City for Hollywood with nothing in his pocket but $40 and one completed animated short subject. He joined his brother Roy in California, where they pooled their resources and set up an animation studio in a small store.

With growing success, they were able to move to a larger studio, where Mickey Mouse was born. He made his film debut in 1928 in "Steamboat Willie," the first sound cartoon, and launched the full-scale production of Disney cartoons. Less than ten years later, "Snow White and the Seven Dwarfs," the world's first full-length animated feature, premiered at the Carthay Circle Theatre in Los Angeles in 1937. The film is still considered one of the great feats of motion pictures. During the next five years, Walt completed several more full-length animated classics, including "Pinocchio," "Fantasia," "Dumbo" and "Bambi."

Walt Disney may have done more to touch the hearts and minds of millions of Americans than any other man in the past century. He brought joy, happiness, and a universal means of communication to people of all nations. Certainly, our world shall know but one Walt Disney.

AMERICA SINGS…After more than two years in the making, America Sings, a comical, tune-filled adventure tracing nearly 200 years of our nation's musical heritage, opened July 29, 1974. Here, the final dress rehearsal is conducted in the "Down South" sequence of the show, as some of the 114 "Audio-Animatronics" "stars" are put through their paces by Disney computer programmers. At WED Enterprises, a sculptor works on a clay sculpture of the owl, while using the smaller scale as a reference.

…LAUGHS…That old hobo Red Skelton was caught "clowning" around with some of Disneyland's "Kids of the Kingdom" while at the Magic Kingdom taping a television special.

Two more funny men, Bob Newhart and Don Rickles, posed momentarily with fellow comedian, Mickey Mouse.

…AND CELEBRATES…

Conceived as a salute and celebration honoring the American Bicentennial, "America on Parade" began its daily performances in July, 1975, at both Disneyland and Walt Disney World, and continued until September 1976. In all, the red, white and blue procession completed more than 1200 performances before a total audience of 25 million people, the largest audience ever to view a live performance.

This 1939 comic book cover provided the inspiration for "America on Parade's" patriotic trio.

Japan's Emperor Hirohito enjoys a performance of "America on Parade."

THE RETURN VISIT OF TWO VERY SPECIAL PEOPLE...
On its 20th Anniversary, Disneyland welcomed back Christine Vess Watkins and her cousin Michael Schwartner who, at ages five and seven, had been the first visitors to enter the Magic Kingdom.

CHAMPIONS OF EVERY SIZE...World champion gymnast, Nadia Comaneci, left her usual serious demeanor behind during her visit to the Magic Kingdom. Opposing Rose Bowl teams have visited Disneyland each year since the late 1950's. Before the January 1, 1976 kickoff, U.S.C. football stars Lynn Swann and Anthony Davis show a few other "characters" how it's done.

ANYTHING CAN HAPPEN AT DISNEYLAND...Spectacular Christmas celebrations are nothing new at Disneyland, but 1976 was the first year the Magic Kingdom found snow on the ground. As part of Sandy Duncan's Christmas special, taped for television at Disneyland, Mickey and Minnie glide gracefully across a frostbitten Main Street.

A "PEAK" INTO THE FUTURE...

"Anyone can build a roller coaster, outside, with a steel frame and cars going up and down and around it; Disney built a 'Space Mountain'."

NEW WEST MAGAZINE

Dedicated on May 27, 1977 in Tomorrowland, Space Mountain opened its portals to Disneyland guests for a most incredible thrill experience, housed within a "Disneysphere" of technological and theatrical treats for the imagination.

Although the concept for Space Mountain came from Walt Disney himself in the mid-1960's, the computer technology needed to build the attraction wasn't developed then. After 12 years of planning, $20 million (more than Walt spent to build the entire Park in 1955) and over a million man-hours in design and construction, the 118-foot tall, 200-foot wide, cone-shaped superstructure

emerged on the Tomorrowland skyline. Because of its enormous size, special consideration had to be made for the design of Space Mountain. Its foundation was built 15 feet below ground surface to make sure that it would fit the existing scale of Disneyland's other structures.

Space Mountain, like other Disney attractions, was designed to be a total "sight and sound experience"; to put people in the middle of a viscerally believable drama. Walt realized that the entire universe could be explored by a device not exclusive to the world of astronomers and space scientists... the vehicle of the mind.

AMERICA'S SPACEMEN CHALK UP ANOTHER "FIRST"...On hand for the Opening Ceremonies in 1977, some of the original seven U.S. astronauts pose together before taking the inaugural ride. Left to right: Gordon Cooper, Wally Schirra, Scott Carpenter and Alan Shepard.

The Tomorrowland space adventure represents some of the most sophisticated technology yet incorporated into a Disneyland attraction. Here "astronauts" of all ages prepare to "blast off" from the Space Port loading area.

MICKEY'S 50! In November of 1978, Disneyland guests were invited to the biggest, brightest birthday party a mouse ever had! Born on Walt's drawing board in 1928, Mickey had (even though he didn't look it) reached middle age.

UP TO HIS EARS IN MOUSEKETEERS...
Mickey welcomed back Mouseketeers from both the original and new Mickey Mouse Club television shows, including Annette Funicello. Along with other "originals" from the 1950's television show, Annette was instrumental in introducing Disneyland to the world.

**GOODBYE *NATURE'S WONDERLAND*…
HELLO *BIG THUNDER!*** In January of 1977,
the two-acre area of the Nature's Wonderland
attraction began an incredible metamorphosis.
A *new* panorama of towering rock formations was
"appearing" on the western horizon of Frontierland
—Big Thunder Mountain Railroad was moving in!
From start to finish, Big Thunder was a "moun-
tainous" project; over seven years of planning,
two years of construction and $15.8 million
were required to bring this thrilling new adventure
to reality.

Intricate scale models were used to
finalize the show design and serve as
guides for on-site production and
construction.

MOUNTAIN MOVING MAGIC…
As the "mountain" began to grow,
plaster and paint were added to create
"rocks" and "boulders." Huge cranes
were used to hoist the complete upper
buttes (weighing up to 28 tons) into
position atop the massive steel
framework.

AGE BEFORE BEAUTY…
The newly constructed old buildings
and varied rock formations were
given a timeworn appearance
by craftsmen called "agers and
grainers." Their artistry, combined
with authentic mining artifacts and
themed landscaping, recreated the
atmosphere of the Old West
a century ago.

In September, 1979, the gold rush era was reborn in Frontierland, as Big Thunder's mine trains began carrying passengers into the rugged landscapes of the Old West—through foreboding caverns, raging waterfalls, and even an "earthquake" causing an "avalanche"!

*D*ISNEYLAND tickles the heart and teases the imagination of people of all ages from all over the world. It represents the ideals, dreams and hard facts of Walt Disney's own life and work.

During his celebrated career, Walt frequently commented on his philosophy of life, his ideals, dreams and his hope for a better world. The following pages reflect Walt Disney's personal philosophy and feelings about children, the family, the future, nature, love and laughter. His dreams live on and his philosophy, imagination and sensitivity are manifested throughout the Magic Kingdom.

"I wanted something alive, something that could grow, something I could keep plussing with ideas; the Park is that. Not only can I add things but even the trees will keep growing. The things will get more beautiful each year."

"I think what I want Disneyland to be most of all is a happy place—a place where adults and children can experience together some of the wonders of life, of adventure, and feel better because of it."

"You can dream, create, design and build the most wonderful place in the world...but it takes people to make the dream a reality."

"Disneyland is a work of love. We didn't go into Disneyland just with the idea of making money."

"Fantasy, if it's really convincing, can't become dated, for the simple reason that it represents a flight into a dimension that lies beyond the reach of time."

"I don't like formal gardens. I like wild nature. It's just the wilderness instinct in me, I guess."

"The important thing is the family. If you can keep the family together—and that's the backbone of our whole business, catering to families—that's what we hope to do."

"All we ever intended for him or expected of him was that he should continue to make people everywhere chuckle with him and at him. We didn't burden him with any social symbolism, we made him no mouth piece for frustrations or harsh satire. Mickey was simply a little personality assigned to the purposes of laughter."

*"Disneyland is like Alice stepping through the
Looking Glass, to step through the portals of
Disneyland will be like entering another world."*

"I love the nostalgic myself.
I hope we never lose some of
the things of the past."

*"It has that thing—
the imagination, and
the feeling of happy
excitement—I knew
when I was a kid."*

"People sort of live in the dark about things. A lot of young people think the future is closed to them, that everything has been done. This is not so. There are still plenty of avenues to be explored."

"Why do we have to grow up? I know more adults who have the children's approach to life. They're people who don't give a hang what the Joneses do. You see them at Disneyland every time you go there. They are not afraid to be delighted with simple pleasures, and they have a degree of contentment with what life has brought—sometimes it isn't much, either."